CHOKWE

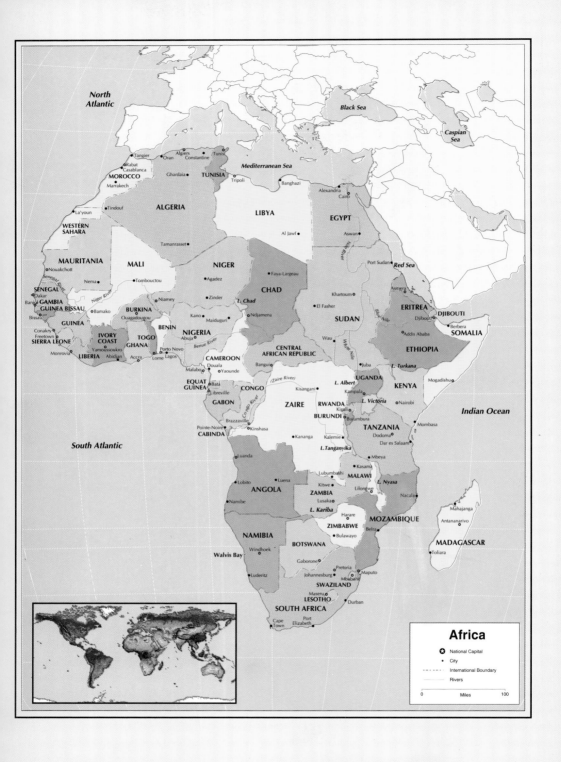

North
Atlantic

Black Sea

Caspian
Sea

Tangier
Algiers • Tunis
Oran • Constantine
Rabat • Mediterranean Sea
Casablanca
MOROCCO
Ghardaia • TUNISIA
Tripoli • Banghazi
Marrakech

Alexandria
Cairo

La'youn • Tindouf
ALGERIA
LIBYA
EGYPT

WESTERN
SAHARA
Al Jawf • Aswan

Tamanrasset •
Port Sudan • Red Sea
MAURITANIA
MALI
NIGER
CHAD
Asmera •

Nouakchott •
Nema •
Faya-Largeau •
ERITREA
DJIBOUTI
SENEGAL
Agadez •
Khartoum •
Djibouti •
Dakar •
Berbera •
GAMBIA
Tombouctou •
Zinder •
El Fasher •
Addis Ababa •
SOMALIA
Banjul
Niamey •
L. Chad
SUDAN
GUINEA BISSAU
BURKINA
Kano •
Ndjamena •
ETHIOPIA
Bissau •
Bamako •
Ouagadougou
Maiduguri •
Wau •
GUINEA
Conakry •
IVORY
BENIN
NIGERIA
Juba •
L. Turkana
Freetown •
COAST
TOGO
Abuja •
CENTRAL
SIERRA LEONE
Yamoussoukro
GHANA
Porto Novo
AFRICAN REPUBLIC
UGANDA
Monrovia •
Abidjan •
Accra • Lagos
Bangui •
L. Albert
KENYA
LIBERIA
Lome
CAMEROON
Kisangani •
Kampala •
Douala •
L. Victoria
Mogadishu •
EQUAT.
Bata • Yaounde •
CONGO
RWANDA
Nairobi •
GUINEA
Libreville •
ZAIRE
Kigali
Malabo •
(Zaire River)
BURUNDI
Indian Ocean
GABON
Bujumbura
Brazzaville •
Mombasa •
Pointe-Noire •
Kinshasa •
Kananga •
TANZANIA
South Atlantic
CABINDA
Kalemie •
Dodoma •
L. Tanganyika
Dar es Salaam •
Luanda •
Mbeya •
Kasama •
Lubumbashi •
MALAWI
Lobito • Luena •
Kitwe •
L. Nyasa
Nacala •
ANGOLA
Lilongwe
ZAMBIA
Lusaka •
Namibe •
L. Kariba
Harare •
MOZAMBIQUE
NAMIBIA
ZIMBABWE
Bulawayo •
Beira •
MADAGASCAR
Mahajanga •
Antananarivo •
BOTSWANA
Walvis Bay
Windhoek •
Gaborone •
Toliara •
Luderitz •
Pretoria •
Johannesburg • Mbabane • Maputo
SWAZILAND
Maseru •
LESOTHO
SOUTH AFRICA
Durban •
Cape • Port
Town Elizabeth

Senegal River
Niger River
Benue River
Congo River
Nile River
Blue Nile
White Nile

Africa

✪ National Capital

• City

- - - - International Boundary

——— Rivers

0   Miles   100

The Heritage Library of African Peoples

CHOKWE

Manuel Jordán, Ph.D.

THE ROSEN PUBLISHING GROUP, INC.
NEW YORK

Published in 1998 by The Rosen Publishing Group, Inc.
29 East 21st Street, New York, NY 10010

First Edition

Manufactured in the United States of America

Library of Congress Cataloging-in-Publication Data

Jordán, Manuel.
    Chokwe / Manuel Jordán. — 1st ed.
      p.   cm. — (The heritage library of African peoples)
    Includes bibliographical references and index.
    Summary: Surveys the history, culture, and contemporary life of
the Chokwe people of Angola, Zaire, and Zimbabwe.
    ISBN 0-8239-1990-0
    1. Chokwe (African people)—History—Juvenile literature.
2. Chokwe (African people)—Social life and customs—Juvenile
literature. [1. Chokwe (African people)] I. Title. II. Series.
DT1308.C67J67   1998
306'.089'96399—dc21   96-50268
                                                                  CIP
                                                                   AC

Contents

INTRODUCTION

THERE IS EVERY REASON FOR US TO KNOW something about Africa and to understand its past and the way of life of its peoples. Africa is a rich continent that has for centuries provided the world with art, culture, labor, wealth, and natural resources. It has vast mineral deposits, fossil fuels, and commercial crops.

But perhaps most important is the fact that fossil evidence indicates that human beings originated in Africa. The earliest traces of human beings and their tools are almost two million years old. Their descendants have migrated throughout the world. To be human is to be of African descent.

The experiences of the peoples who stayed in Africa are as rich and as diverse as of those who established themselves elsewhere. This series of books describes their environment, their modes of subsistence, their relationships, and their customs and beliefs. The books present the variety of languages, histories, cultures, and religions that are to be found on the African continent. They demonstrate the historical linkages between African peoples and the way contemporary Africa has been affected by European colonial rule.

Africa is large, complex, and diverse. It encompasses an area of more than 11,700,000 square miles. The United States, Europe, and India could fit easily into it. The sheer size is an indication of the continent's great variety in geography, terrain, climate, flora, fauna, peoples, languages, and cultures.

Much of contemporary Africa has been shaped by European colonial rule, industrialization, urbanization, and the demands of a world economic system. For more than seventy years, large regions of Africa were ruled by Great Britain, France, Belgium, Portugal, and Spain. African peoples from various ethnic, linguistic, and cultural backgrounds were brought together to form colonial states.

For decades Africans struggled to gain their independence. It was not until after World War II that the colonial territories became independent African states. Today, almost all of Africa is ruled by Africans. Large numbers of Africans live in modern cities. Rural Africa is also being transformed, and yet its people still engage in many of their customs and beliefs.

Contemporary circumstances and natural events have not always been kind to ordinary Africans. Today, however, new popular social movements and technological innovations pose great promise for future development.

George C. Bond, Ph.D., Director
Institute of African Studies
Columbia University, New York

The rich culture of the Chokwe has had a great influence in central Africa. To become adults, Chokwe boys and girls must attend separate initiation camps. Masks used during Chokwe initiations, such as the one seen here, have also been adopted by neighboring peoples. This mask represents an ancestral spirit.

chapter

1

THE LAND AND THE PEOPLE

TO BERNARD MUKUTA SAMUKINJI, A respected specialist in the customs of his people, being Chokwe means being part of a rich history and cultural tradition. This history, Mr. Samukinji explains, can be grasped by looking at the achievements of a long line of powerful Chokwe chiefs. They helped their people overcome enormous difficulties.

The Chokwe have faced more than three centuries of conflict with neighboring peoples and the Portuguese. The Portuguese first visited the coast of this part of Africa in the late 1400s. They became an increasingly powerful political factor in Angola, where most Chokwe live.

In 1885 Angola became a Portuguese colony, ruled by Portugal. For almost a century, the black peoples of Angola resisted Portuguese rule. Widespread violence broke out in 1961.

Because of his expert knowledge of Chokwe tradition, Bernard Mukuta Samukinji (above) is often hired to oversee traditional ceremonies in Chokwe villages. In this picture he is showing the spot he has cleared for the building of a new house.

Angola then plunged into a war of liberation that lasted until 1975, when the Portuguese finally surrendered Angola to the Angolan people. Unfortunately, since that time civil war has continued because various Angolan groups have been competing for power. A peace agreement signed in 1993 eased the conflict but did not bring it to an end entirely.

To explain how the Chokwe are different from neighboring peoples (who have lived in the same region and share similar histories), Mr. Samukinji says, "I am Chokwe and the Chokwe move a lot." By this he does not mean that the Chokwe move around *physically*. Instead he describes the character of the people. The Chokwe are both smart and assertive. To "move" is to actively confront problems so that they can be overcome.

The Chokwe have developed rich cultural traditions, which are reflected in their art. At the height of their political power in the 1800s, the Chokwe created many objects for important

Chokwe art still plays important roles in traditional Chokwe religion. Today fine examples of Chokwe art, such as this wooden sculpture of a woman and child, are found in museums and art collections around the world.

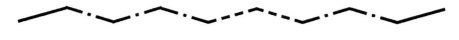

chiefs. The Chokwe still make many types of sculpted figures and masks to honor and contain the spirits of their ancestors. These art objects provide vital links with the past. The Chokwe also hold complex ceremonies that show their world view and religious beliefs. This belief system underlies the strong sense of identity shared by Chokwe such as Mr. Samukinji.

Over 600,000 Chokwe people live in a vast area that spans northeastern, central, and southern Angola (their country of origin) as well as parts of southern Congo and western and northwestern Zambia. The Chokwe speak Kichokwe, which is part of the Bantu group of African languages. The Chokwe's many neighbors include the Lunda, Pende, Mbangani, and Kete to the north; Minungu, Lwena, Luchazi, Mbwela, and Mbunda to the east; Holo, Mbundu, Imbangala, Songo, and Ovimbundu to the west; and the Kwanyama to the south. Most of these ethnic groups have long historic links with the Chokwe. They share many traditions and speak similar languages.

▼ TERRITORY ▼

The lands populated by the Chokwe vary greatly. Dense woodlands and rain forests are found in areas near the Kasai and Kwilu Rivers of Congo and northern Angola. Savanna plains and grasslands cover the Angolan Central

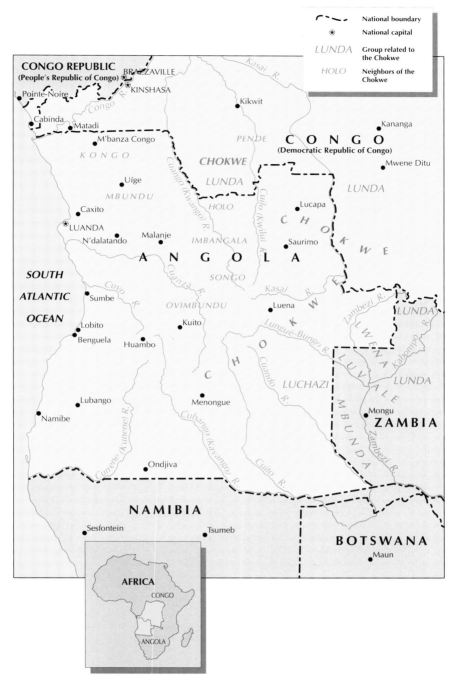

legend:
- - - National boundary
✳ National capital
LUNDA Group related to the Chokwe
HOLO Neighbors of the Chokwe

CONGO REPUBLIC
(People's Republic of Congo)
BRAZZAVILLE ✳
✳ KINSHASA

Pointe-Noire

Cabinda
Matadi
M'banza Congo

KONGO

PENDE

CONGO
(Democratic Republic of Congo)

Kikwit

Kananga

Mwene Ditu

Uíge

MBUNDU

Caxito

✳LUANDA
N'dalatando   Malanje

CHOKWE

LUNDA

HOLO

IMBANGALA

Lucapa

C
H
O

Saurimo

K
W
E

LUNDA

A N G O L A

SONGO

Kasai R.

OVIMBUNDU

Luena

C
H
O
K
W
E

LUNDA

Zambezi R.

LWENA

LUVALE

LUNDA

SOUTH
ATLANTIC
OCEAN

Sumbe

Kuito

Lobito
Benguela   Huambo

C

LUCHAZI

M
B
U
N
D
A

Mongu

ZAMBIA

Lubango

Namibe

H
O
K

Menongue

Ondjiva

NAMIBIA

Sesfontein   Tsumeb

BOTSWANA

Maun

AFRICA

CONGO

ANGOLA

The Chokwe are found mainly in Angola, with smaller populations in
Congo and western Zambia.

Today the Chokwe live in both rural and urban environments, such as along the Zambezi River (above) and in Luanda, the capital city of Angola (below).

Plateau, extending east of the Zambezi River in Zambia. The land in southeastern Angola and western Zambia has sandy soil and floodplains near the Kwando and the Zambezi rivers.

▼ CLIMATE ▼

The climate in Angola, Congo, and Zambia is marked by two distinct seasons: a rainy season that begins around October and ends in April; and a dry season, with little rainfall, during the rest of the year. The rainy season is warmer, with temperatures rising above ninety degrees Fahrenheit. The dry season is cooler; temperatures drop below sixty degrees at night.

The weather plays a large role in village life. People farm, hunt, fish, and build houses according to the change of seasons. Most Chokwe plan traditional ceremonies during the dry season.▲

2

VILLAGE LIFE

A Chokwe village consists of houses where relatives of a village headman, or chief, live with their families. A village headman normally owns the largest house, which he shares with his wife. Village headmen often have more than one wife. Each wife lives in her own house along with her children. A headman's first wife is considered senior to the others and she is normally in charge of distributing shared goods, such as the family's food, to the other wives.

Chokwe houses are generally built in a large circle around a shared open yard. In the center of the yard a large tree can be found. People can enjoy its shade during the hot afternoon hours. A common feature in Chokwe villages is the *chota* shelter. A *chota* has a cone-shaped grass roof set on a structure of freestanding wooden

Traditional Chokwe architecture uses temporary materials. The men seen here are thatching the roof of a rural home.

poles. Built in the center of a yard, the *chota* is the place where visitors are received and where men meet. Other structures found in Chokwe villages are storage rooms and kitchens, both of which are built next to the houses.

Chokwe houses are made from sun-dried mud bricks. These mud bricks can be either bought or made at home in wooden molds. To build a Chokwe house, men pile up the bricks to make walls, using mud as a mortar to hold the bricks together. A structure made from poles and reeds is then placed on top of the walls to support a thatched roof. A layer of thick grass tied up in bunches is placed on the roof. Extra

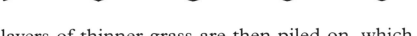

layers of thinner grass are then piled on, which protect the house during the rainy seasons.

Houses are repaired during the dry season by adding extra mud to the walls and layers of grass to the roofs. People who know they will be staying in a certain place only for a short time build less permanent houses with reed or grass walls. Because all of the houses are built of natural materials, they collapse shortly after people leave them.

At the beginning of the dry season, areas near villages are cleared for farming. The Chokwe also set aside farmlands miles away from their homes. They grow corn, cassava, and millet, the staples of the Chokwe diet. In addition, a variety of vegetables, including sweet potatoes, pumpkins, tomatoes, okra, and in some areas, high-protein foods, such as rice, beans, and peanuts, are grown.

The Chokwe also raise cattle, goats, pigs, and chickens. They eat these animals only on special occasions, such as wedding feasts. Artificial beehives are placed in the forests for harvesting honey and beeswax. These items are kept or traded for other goods. Chokwe who live near rivers also fish to supplement their diets. Men usually fish with lines and hooks or with nets from dugout canoes. Women fish from the riverbanks using large baskets to catch the fish.

Hunting is a traditional Chokwe occupation, but modern laws against poaching have restricted most forms of hunting in Zambia. All people are required to purchase hunting permits, which few rural people can afford. As a result, many feel that the hunting laws are unjust and break with Chokwe traditions. The Chokwe and their neighbors often ignore the law and continue to hunt. The main catch is antelope, which they share with their families or sell or trade to other villages.

Chokwe men hunt with guns or bows and arrows. They hunt alone or in groups. Boys learn hunting techniques during their initiation ceremonies. This is where they learn most matters related to their future roles as adults. For the Chokwe, hunting is closely related to religious beliefs. They often build shrines to pay respect to ancestors who were successful hunters during their lifetimes.

▼ FREE TIME ▼

The Chokwe find the time to enjoy the company of relatives and friends and to share all sorts of personal stories. While relaxing, people usually fix their tools, carve new household objects such as spoons and handles, and weave baskets or mats. At the town market people can meet with friends who live in other villages. Those who return from the market

In rural areas craft work is done when there is free time from farming. Maria Chitofu, seen here, weaves baskets from fibers and other natural materials.

usually have many stories to tell about people they met there.

During the evening, people often sit around fires and tell stories. Traditional Chokwe stories usually have a moral and help to teach values that benefit the community, especially children.

On the nights of the full moon, children and young adults sing together, dance, and make music by using stools as drums and hitting glass bottles with sticks. Their songs often have a brief message about a particular story or experience. Songs may comment on love, discuss the civil war in Angola, or mention the accomplishments of sports figures. Some Chokwe youths listen to the international news on their radios. They spread the news in their communities by singing songs about the news stories. One popular song celebrates the fame and success of Maradona, the soccer player from Argentina.

Children enjoy a variety of games and activities. They draw pictures in the sand, make their own dolls or trucks, invent musical instruments, or play soccer with balls made of old rags. Children spend a lot of time playing, but they also must help with chores. Chokwe teens are given their own small fields to farm. A combination of work and play prepares them for their adult responsibilities.

THE TRICKSTER RABBIT AND THE WISE TURTLE

(From a story told by children of the Chitofu village in Zambia)

There was hunger in the animal world. A group of animals decided to gather food together and store it in a camp where it could be shared by all. Each day a different animal was chosen to guard the food in the camp while the others went to find more food.

Across the river from the animal camp lived a rabbit who had a canoe, a fishing hook, and a drum. One day the rabbit decided to try to steal food from the animal camp. He arrived at the camp with a fish he had caught and his drum. The zebra guarding the camp welcomed him. The rabbit asked the zebra to cook the fish while he played the drum. But the zebra decided to dance to the drum music instead of watching the fish.

When the fish started to burn the rabbit asked, "Where is the fish that I gave you to cook?" The zebra said it was ruined. The rabbit challenged the zebra to a fight because of the ruined fish. "You are too little to fight me," said the zebra. The rabbit grabbed the zebra's legs and tied them up. He stole all the food from the camp and went back across the river. The other animals returned from gathering food and found the zebra tied up and all of the food gone.

The next day, the rabbit came to the camp again, with another fish and his drum. This time an elephant was guarding the camp. Like the zebra, the elephant was fooled by the rabbit's politeness. The elephant danced while the rabbit played the drum. Once again the fish burned and the rabbit told the elephant they would have to fight because he had wasted the rabbit's fish. "You are too little to fight me," said the elephant.

And once again the other animals returned from gathering food and found the elephant tied up and all of the food gone.

Day after day the same thing happened until one day the turtle was left to guard the camp. The turtle made a stool with a hole in the seat. The turtle prepared a meal and placed it by the fire. He hid under the stool holding a needle. The wise turtle was ready for the rabbit!

Once again the rabbit arrived with a fish and his drum, but this time he found the camp empty. When he called out, nobody answered. The rabbit then washed his hands and sat on the stool to eat the food that the turtle had placed by the fire. The turtle, still hiding under the stool, poked the needle through the hole. The startled rabbit jumped in pain. The rabbit inspected the stool, but could find nothing wrong with it. Confused, the rabbit sat down again — and the turtle pushed the needle through the hole again. The turtle crawled out from under the stool, seized the rabbit's tail in his mouth, and held him captive.

The other animals returned from gathering food and were very surprised that the turtle had captured the rabbit. The elephant told the rabbit he would be punished for fooling the other animals. They threatened to throw the rabbit high up in the air. The rabbit said, "If you really want to hurt me, tell your friends to gather some sand, so that when you throw me up in the air, I will fall down in the sand, which is bad for rabbits." The animals believed the rabbit and threw him up in the air to fall in the sand. The sand softened the rabbit's fall so he did not get hurt. When he landed, he grabbed some sand from the ground and threw it into the other animals' eyes. The rabbit escaped without being punished, but he realized the wisdom of the turtle and decided not to steal anymore.

▼ VILLAGE COURTS ▼

Most Chokwe territories have at least three types of legal organizations: the village courts, the chiefs' courts, and the district courts. Some districts have their own police forces and legal courts to settle legal cases, but in many rural areas the law is upheld in village and chiefs' courts. In village courts, respected male elders oversee cases involving land ownership, family quarrels, theft, and disputes in which witchcraft is suspected. A village headman usually leads the village court.

During a village court session, the male elders sit together on one side of the open yard. Female elders sit on the other side. The parties involved in the conflict sit in the middle, where they explain their situations one at a time. Usually an audience gathers to listen. The individuals and the witnesses involved in the disputes are asked direct questions. A decision is made by court agreement. Guilty individuals are instructed to apologize and may have to pay fees of goods or money or to repair the damages they have caused.

Senior chiefs and their court officers listen to disputes that could not be settled in the village. If necessary, a chief may send a delegation of court officials to a village to hear a particular case. The village chief will accept the judgment of these officials.

If a person is not happy with the village court's decision, he or she may also decide to go directly to a chief's court, where the decision of the village court is reviewed.

Criminal cases and serious financial disputes are usually taken to district courts.▲

chapter

3

CHOKWE HISTORY

THE ORIGIN OF THE CHOKWE AS AN ETHNIC group can be traced to the migrations of the Lunda people in the 1600s. Varied and sometimes contradictory accounts explain how a Lunda kingdom from the north came to occupy what is now southern Congo.

At the end of the 1500s, the Lunda in northern Congo were ruled by a senior chief named Konde. Konde had two sons, Chinguli and Chinyama, and a daughter known as Lweji. Konde had to decide which of his sons was better suited to inherit his throne. The brothers' constant arguments and distrust of their father forced Konde to ignore the Lunda tradition of passing power from father to son. Instead he named his more mature daughter, Lweji, as his successor. Lweji became the first female Lunda chief.

In what has been called a Lunda love story,
Lweji met a hunter of royal Luba blood named
Chibinda Ilunga. Impressed with his courtly
manners and outstanding hunting abilities, Lweji
eventually married him. Chibinda Ilunga introduced the bow and arrow to Lunda country.
Soon after his marriage, Chibinda Ilunga
became the new Lunda ruler.

Chinguli and Chinyama were upset by
Konde's decision to name Lweji chief and by
the events that led Chibinda Ilunga, a foreigner,
to acquire that title. They decided to migrate.
Chinguli, Chinyama, and their followers finally
set up new chiefdoms, far to the southwest.
They achieved this by mixing with the local pop-
ulations that they encountered in central Angola.
The Chokwe, Lwena, Luchazi, Mbundu, and
other ethnic groups trace their origins to the
Lunda migrations led by Chinguli and
Chinyama in the early 1600s.

Although the original Chokwe group developed independently of the Lunda, Chokwe
chiefs remained under the political authority of
the Lunda supreme chief. Chokwe chiefs were
required to pay tribute and taxes to the Lunda
supreme chief.

Beginning in the 1600s, the Chokwe traded
goods on the commercial routes connecting the
Angolan interior to the coast. Colonized by the
Portuguese, Angola has long been a center for

For almost three centuries the Chokwe fell under the authority of the Lunda, with whom they continue to share many traditions. Seen here is Nyakulenga, the female chief of the southern Lunda in northwestern Zambia. She is being carried by members of her court during a public ceremony.

trade between African groups and between Africans and Europeans. The Chokwe traded with their Imbangala and Ovimbundu neighbors to the west for ivory, rubber, and beeswax. In this way, the Chokwe were able to meet the Portuguese demand for these goods. The Portuguese also needed workers for their mines and plantations. For this reason, both the Chokwe and the Portuguese took part in the slave trade and slave raids in neighboring lands. The Chokwe supplied the Portuguese with slaves from their territory in exchange for European goods and weapons. The Chokwe became very wealthy by participating in the trade routes.

The Chokwe increased their land holdings to the north and south, and soon controlled vast areas of central Angola. In 1887 the Chokwe invaded the Lunda capital in Congo, putting an end to Lunda political influence over Chokwe matters. The Chokwe have since had their own paramount (supreme) chief called the Mwachisenge. Even so, they still recognize their Lunda origins and respect the political structures of their Lunda neighbors and relatives.▲

chapter

4

RELIGION

THE CHOKWE BELIEVE IN A SUPREME BEING
that they call Kalunga or Nzambi. Kalunga is
mentioned in prayers, and in the Chokwe lan-
guage the name itself has come to mean great-
ness. For example, the Chokwe term for ocean is
kalungalwiji, which means great river, or river of
God. Although the Chokwe have a rich artistic
tradition, they do not paint or carve images of
Kalunga. This shows their great respect for the
Supreme Being.

A Chokwe chief is regarded as the represen-
tative of God on Earth. This belief is known as
sacred kingship. Sacred kingship was introduced
by the royal Luba hunter Chibinda Ilunga.

Chokwe ancestors are viewed as inter-
mediaries between God and humans. Most
human concerns are directed through the
ancestors.

▼ ANCESTRAL SPIRITS ▼

Success or failure in life is directly related to a person's relationship with his or her ancestors. These ancestral spirits are known as *mahamba*. The spirits have a two-sided nature: they can either help or harm their descendants, depending upon whether they have been honored or neglected by their living relatives.

The Chokwe build ancestral shrines to honor their ancestors. Inside the shrines, they place sculptures, objects, and artifacts. These are meant to contain or represent the spirits or to serve as points of contact between living people and spiritual forces. At these shrines, called *kachipango*, the Chokwe invoke, or call, their ancestral spirits. They offer both prayers and gifts to honor the memory of their dead relatives.

Certain types of trees, termite mounds, and even the oldest houses in some villages are seen as gateways for the ancestors. Through these places ancestors can pass from the world of the dead into the world of the living. People also make offerings to the ancestors in these spiritual places.

▼ HEALERS AND DIVINERS ▼

Chokwe traditional healers, known as *mbuki* or *chimbanda*, use a variety of medicines to treat the diseases from which their patients suffer. Healers have great knowledge of the medicinal

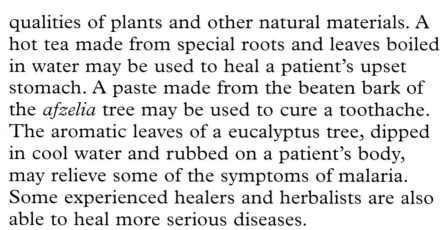

qualities of plants and other natural materials. A hot tea made from special roots and leaves boiled in water may be used to heal a patient's upset stomach. A paste made from the beaten bark of the *afzelia* tree may be used to cure a toothache. The aromatic leaves of a eucalyptus tree, dipped in cool water and rubbed on a patient's body, may relieve some of the symptoms of malaria. Some experienced healers and herbalists are also able to heal more serious diseases.

In cases of recurring illness or misfortune among individuals or whole communities, it is the job of a diviner, or *tahi*, to reveal the source or cause of the problem. The Chokwe believe that diviners have the power to channel the spiritual or supernatural forces that affect people's lives. Diviners serve as go-betweens for humans and spirits.

Although disease, bad luck, and death may be considered natural occurrences, the Chokwe believe that evildoers or angry ancestors may be responsible for these and all sorts of other problems. A diviner's duty is to determine whether a patient is suffering from a common illness or one caused by an upset ancestor. Once a diviner identifies the problem, the patient can appeal to his or her ancestors and honor them in order to regain health.

Some people in Chokwe society have evil intentions and choose to create conflict and disharmony for all members of their communities. The Chokwe believe that these individuals can use supernatural powers to harm others without harming themselves. With the aid of their guardian ancestral spirits, Chokwe diviners are able to see the plans of individuals with evil intentions, who are known as witches (*nganga* or *uloji*). Only powerful diviners are capable of successfully confronting them. Being a witch is sometimes considered a disease that attacks an individual, so diviners may prescribe medicines and other methods to help the person return to his or her normal self.

Chokwe diviners specialize in channeling the spiritual and supernatural forces that people believe shape their lives. Seen here is Mr. Chipoya, a diviner who died in 1993 after a fifty-year career in divination.

ANIMAL SYMBOLISM

Images of wild animals such as birds, bats, rabbits, baboons, lions, aardvarks, and pangolins (anteaters), as well as domestic dogs and pigs, are found in Chokwe art. Animal parts — furs, feathers, claws, beaks, and bones — are often used to decorate divination costumes.

The behavior and extraordinary abilities of certain animals can serve as models for humans. A Chokwe chief might be called a lion because he wishes to be associated with the power and regal qualities of that animal. A chief may also use images of bats as symbols of his authority. These symbols suggest to people that, like the bat, the chief can fly at night and be aware of everything that happens in his territory.

Similarly, diviners may keep the furs of genets (nocturnal wildcats) to suggest that they have the ability to move at night and discover the hidden intentions of evildoers. A genet is a fast and shy creature. Rarely seen, genets seem to vanish as soon as they are spotted. The Chokwe associate the genets' ability to escape from sight with invisibility. They believe that the owner of a genet fur can become invisible to others.

Dogs are also important because of their speed. They help their owners catch game during hunting trips. The Chokwe also believe that dogs have the ability to see things that are invisible to humans. When people are asleep in the village and dogs begin to howl, dogs are supposedly warning their owners about invisible beings. Because dogs faithfully guard their owners, they are highly revered by the Chokwe.

Baboons are admired because they behave like humans. Baboons have families. Female baboons treat their offspring with the same care a human mother treats her own baby. Baboons are therefore considered to be related to humans.

Aardvarks and pangolins (scaly anteaters) are special because they live underground. The Chokwe believe that these animals are in contact with the ancestors in the underworld. The Chokwe name for a pangolin is *nkaka*, the same word for grandfather.

According to Chokwe tradition, the pangolin (above) is a spiritually significant animal, closely related to the ancestors. One reason for the symbolic importance of pangolins is that they live underground, where the ancestors are buried. When alarmed, pangolins, which range from three to six feet in length, roll up into a tight ball with their scales sticking out like a pine cone.

Diviners may also resolve disputes in their communities. Some diviners have such good reputations that clients travel hundreds of miles to benefit from their services.

▼ DIVINATION TOOLS ▼

To contact a guardian ancestral spirit or to receive a message about a patient's condition, a diviner uses a divination tool called *ngombo*. The most elaborate type of *ngombo* is called *ngombo ya chisuka* or *ngombo ya kusekula*. This divination tool is a round, shallow basket filled with different objects. Called *tupele*, these objects include carved wooden figurines, animal parts, seeds, shells, rocks, pieces of glass, ceramics, and other materials. A divination basket may contain over a hundred *tupele*, which symbolize all aspects of life.

Although diviners may be male or female, basket divination is used only by men. During a basket divination session, a diviner will shake and toss the objects within the basket until his guardian spirit instructs him to stop. The diviner will then "read" the pattern of fallen objects, which contains a message about the patient's problem. The diviner then discusses his findings with the patient. Every time the patient asks a question about his or her condition, the diviner gives the basket another shake. The divination process may last over an hour, depending on the patient's condition.

Professional diviners charge their patients standard fees for divination sessions. Diviners rarely practice full time. Instead, they spend most of their time farming or doing chores like other Chokwe people.

Diviners play a key role in Chokwe society. They often become successful village chiefs because of their extraordinary ability to help people overcome difficult problems.▲

chapter

5

CHOKWE INITIATION

TO BECOME ADULT MEMBERS OF CHOKWE society, boys and girls are expected to attend initiation camps. Males enter initiation camp at puberty. Their process of initiation is called *mukanda*.

Females have an equivalent initiation camp called *ukule*. Both initiations take place in secluded places. The matters taught in these camps are considered the exclusive knowledge of initiated men and women.

▼ *MUKANDA* (MALE INITIATION) ▼

For *mukanda*, an enclosure with tall grass walls is built in a private place in the woods away from the village. All initiates, called *tundanji*, are circumcised there. This is the first Chokwe requirement for manhood. The initiates remain in or near the *mukanda* camp until the end of

Initiates remain secluded in their special enclosure for as long as one year. During this time they are supervised by adult men. Seen here are four initiates, kneeling, together with their supervisors.

the initiation process. There, the boys remain under the supervision of caretakers, or *vilombola*. *Mukanda* may last from a couple of months to a year. The initiates are not allowed to return to the village or to approach women or uninitiated members of society until they graduate.

Village elders and caretakers educate the initiates on matters such as religion, morals, sexuality, and technology. The initiation period is viewed as a symbolic death of the initiates' childhood. At graduation, the initiates are "reborn" as adult members of Chokwe society.

▼ *MUKANDA* MASKS ▼

To ensure a successful initiation, Chokwe ask their ancestors for help. Their spirits "come to life" in the form of masks. The Chokwe create many different types of masks, or *mukishi*. These masks take on human, animal, or abstract forms and qualities. Some *mukishi* are meant to entertain and celebrate the occasion of *mukanda*. Other masks serve to protect the initiation camp from intruders.

A mask called Chihongo has male human features carved out of wood. It represents an ancestral Chokwe chief. Chihongo is marked by a crown of fibers and feathers attached to its head and a protruding disc on its chin that represents a chief's beard. The female counterpart to Chihongo is Pwo or Pwevo, a *mukishi* that represents the beauty and wisdom of women. A man and a woman wearing Chihongo and Pwo masks may dance together in performances. Members of

This mask, called Pwo, honors the beauty and wisdom of women.

the community play drums, clap their hands, sing, and dance to celebrate the visit of their ancestors. Chihongo and Pwo represent ideals of male and female beauty and behavior, and their dances teach social and moral lessons.

Whereas Chihongo and Pwo represent positive role models, other masks such as Ndondo (the fool) and Ngulu (the pig) represent negative role models. Ndondo is a man with a big belly who is dressed in ragged clothes and behaves stupidly. Ndondo begs for money and threatens the audience with weapons during performances. Ngulu represents a domestic pig, and its

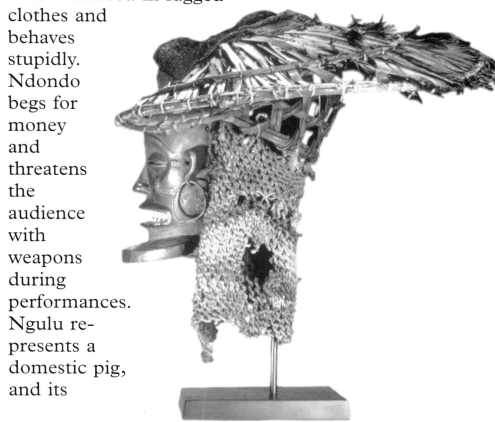

The mask seen here is called Chihongo. It represents a Chokwe chief.

Chikuza, seen here, is one of the most important Chokwe
masks. Regarded as extremely powerful, Chikuza protects the
initiation camp both physically and spiritually. Chikuza also
promotes human fertility and success in hunting.

performance imitates the foolish behavior often associated with the animal.

The silly behavior of Ndondo and Ngulu contrasts with the beautiful manners of Chihongo and Pwo. The message conveyed by these masks is that every Chokwe should act with the composure of Chihongo and Pwo and not act stupidly or irrationally, like Ndondo and Ngulu.

One of the most important initiation masks for the Chokwe is Chikuza. Chikuza has a tall, cone-shaped head. This mask is not carved in wood but built from a frame of twigs and bent branches. Bark cloth and beeswax or tar are added to make facial features and head details. Chikuza's main role is to protect the initiation camp physically and spiritually. Chikuza also has supernatural powers that are associated with human fertility and good luck in hunting. Miniature carved Chikuza figurines are used as amulets, or good-luck charms, by hunters and by women who suffer from infertility.

According to a Zambian diviner named Sasombo, Chikuza's association with fertility began with the story of a well-known Chokwe *mukishi* dancer. The Chokwe man was the best Chikuza performer in his territory. The dancer adopted his two granddaughters, Jinga and Chisola, after the girls' parents died. While the girls were still young, the grandfather became very ill. Before his death, the Chikuza dancer

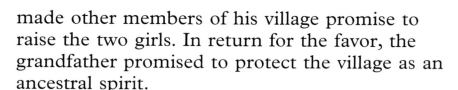

made other members of his village promise to raise the two girls. In return for the favor, the grandfather promised to protect the village as an ancestral spirit.

The girls grew up healthy and happy. Since then, Chikuza has been associated with fertility and growth. Today Chokwe and related peoples still use two types of amulets called *jinga* and *chisola* (the names of the two girls) to help women who have trouble conceiving children.

Because of their rich symbolism and supernatural qualities, Chikuza and all masks play significant roles in Chokwe *mukanda*. Important social, religious, and cultural values are taught through performances featuring these masks.

During *mukanda* graduation ceremonies, all the *mukishi* perform to honor the new initiates. The initiates are decorated with body paint and dressed in grass skirts and hats. After the *mukishi* performance, the initiates are brought back to their villages. There they perform dances that mark their transition into adult life.

▼ *UKULE* (FEMALE INITIATION) ▼

The female initiation is called *ukule* (*mwali* in Zambia). This name describes both the initiation camp itself and the related events through which young women pass into adulthood. Although *mukishi* usually appear only at male initiations, women sometimes mime *mukishi*

Mukanda graduation ceremonies are among the most important and joyful Chokwe celebrations. Graduates, such as the boy seen on the front cover of this book, are dressed in special costumes for their return to the village. Their mothers, grandmothers, and sisters decorate their hair with beads and flowers, as seen in these pictures. In the picture at top left, a young mother with her baby on her back watches the events of the ceremony. In the bottom picture, a woman sings to welcome and praise the graduates. She also waves a fly whisk, made from the tail of an animal, to send blessings through the air.

dances to protect their initiation campgrounds from intruders.

While boys undergo *mukanda* as a group, girls are initiated individually during *ukule*. They require individual education to prepare them for marriage soon after *ukule* ends.

While boys are normally seven to twelve years old when initiated, female initiates are older than thirteen. At this time a girl's mother, grandmothers, and elder sisters organize a series of ceremonial lessons to prepare her for womanhood. These lessons honor the family's ancestors and show the physical and mental changes the girl will undergo.

The *ukule* camp is built on the outskirts of the village. A small cone-shaped grass hut called a *nkunka* is erected within the camp. This is where the initiates sleep and spend their evening hours. The initiation period may last from a couple of weeks to a few months. During this time, the initiate's instructors supervise her.

To beautify an initiate's body and prepare it for birth, a specialist scarifies her abdomen and lower back. These decorative scars are made by first cutting the skin, then rubbing in ashes. The scars that form in the raised areas of the skin are considered beautiful by the Chokwe.

The initiates receive intensive instruction about sexual matters and motherhood. After *ukule*, the initiates are ready for marriage. The

During *ukule*, female initiation, the girls sleep inside a cone-shaped hut called the *nkunka* (above).

At their graduation from *ukule*, young women return to the village in a column, accompanied by relatives. Like those of the young men, the women's bodies are painted with white designs (above).

initiates are expected to have many children which will ensure the continuity of the Chokwe.

At the end of *ukule*, the initiate is decorated with body paint in linear designs. A young girl assists the initiate, wears similar decorations, and walks with her in a procession to the village grounds. Family members accompany the procession to the village, where music and dances are performed to celebrate the occasion.

At the village, the *ukule* initiate performs dances she learned during her initiation and receives gifts from her relatives and neighbors. The ceremony ends the initiation and marks the initiate's transition to adulthood.

▼ ADULT INITIATION ▼

In addition to the required *mukanda* and *ukule* initiations for boys and girls, Chokwe adults may become members of secret societies through an initiation process. The male *mungonge* association and the female *chiwila* association help adults make contact with Chokwe ancestors. In the camps held for these associations, initiates gain special knowledge of ideas related to the supernatural world. Both male and female initiates undergo intensive mental and physical drills which are aimed at building character, strength, and endurance.

CHIKISHIKISHI: THE MASK SPIRIT

Chokwe and related peoples tell stories both to have fun and to teach lessons. These stories often describe extraordinary meetings between humans and spirits. The following story by Arone and Freddy Chitofu is an example of one such encounter.

Chikishikishi, the bush spirit mask, decided to find himself a human wife. He traveled through the bush until he reached a village. There he transformed himself into a human. To impress the villagers he dressed up in a suit and tie and carried a briefcase. As he entered the village, he met a group of young girls playing together. Chikishikishi asked if they knew of a good woman for him to marry. One of the girls said that she had an elder sister who was both beautiful and hard working. The girl took Chikishikishi home to meet her sister.

Chikishikishi met the woman's family, paid the bride-price (a payment made by the groom to the bride's family) and left with his new wife. As is customary, the younger sister accompanied the couple for a few days to make sure the marriage was a good decision. When the three had walked for a few miles, Chikishikishi told his wife that he did not want her younger sister to follow them. His wife told the girl to return home. But the girl was afraid something bad would happen to her elder sister, so she decided to follow them anyway. Chikishikishi and his wife arrived at his home and realized the girl had been following them all along. They had to let her stay. Chikishikishi's mother, who had also turned herself into a human, received the visitors and cooked a meal for them.

One day Chikishikishi told his wife he was going to visit some friends. He did not return that night. The following morning, the girl ventured out into the bush to eat wild fruits. There she met an old woman who asked the girl to help remove some parasites from her body. The girl helped the old lady. In gratitude, the woman warned the girl that Chikishikishi was not human and that he planned to eat the girl and her sister.

That evening Chikishikishi returned, but the girl had barred the door so that he could not enter their house. In the morning Chikishikishi left before dawn. His wife, still unaware of Chikishikishi's intentions, complained to her mother-in-law that she did not like sleeping without

her husband. She feared that a mask might come and eat her and her sister. The mother-in-law told her that had already happened to Chikishikishi's first wife.

Overhearing this and realizing the danger, the girl went back to the old woman for help. The woman told the girl to return to the house, cut some wood, and build a large chicken coop on the roof. The girl was told to enter the coop with her sister and say out loud, "My brother-in-law, stay well because we are leaving." After doing this, the girl and her sister could fly back to their village inside the magical chicken coop. The girl finally convinced her sister of the danger. They did exactly as the old woman said and arrived safely back home.

The moment Chikishikishi returned home, his mother told him what had happened. Not wanting to be outwitted, Chikishikishi decided to pursue them.

The girl explained to the villagers that her sister had mistakenly married a spirit mask and not a man, and that Chikishikishi was probably on his way to retrieve his bride. The girl's father organized the villagers. They made a pitfall trap by digging a pit into the kitchen floor. They lined the bottom with spears and covered the hole with a mat.

Chikishikishi arrived at the village dressed in a suit, carrying a briefcase. He was received by his father-in-law, who offered him a stool, and asked him to sit in a *chota* shelter. A chicken was killed and a meal prepared for him. When it was ready, his wife called him into the kitchen to eat and invited him to sit on the mat. Chikishikishi fell onto the spear points in the pit and died. He was buried in that same hole.

This dramatic story presents social and moral values shared by the Chokwe and related peoples. A person should help those in need, even if it means cleaning parasites off an elder's body. By helping the old woman, the girl found out how to escape from Chikishikishi. The power of unity is shown by the community joining forces to kill the mask. The main theme of this story, however, is that appearances can be deceptive. A person must be cautious, for no one really knows what the hidden intentions of others may be. When in doubt or in need, seeking help from family and friends is a good idea.

The *mungonge* and *chiwila* graduates are sworn to keep the secrets of their associations. Initiation into these societies gives Chokwe men and women access to extraordinary knowledge. The graduates are greatly respected by other community members.

Although some Chokwe communities continue to perform *mungonge* and *chiwila* initiations, these practices have become less common. The initiation customs of *mukanda* and *ukule*, however, continue to be key cultural requirements for all Chokwe.▲

chapter

6

THE CHOKWE TODAY

THE FACT THAT CHOKWE TERRITORIES ARE far inland helped the Chokwe avoid Portuguese colonial influence until the 1600s. Their neighbors to the west — the Imbangala, the Mbundu, and the Ovimbundu — were closer to the coast and suffered more directly under colonial rule. The relationship between the Chokwe and the Portuguese was complex. Sometimes the Chokwe fought the Portuguese; at other times they became allies. This is similar to the Chokwe's relationship with their Lunda neighbors and relatives.

The Chokwe developed and maintained their cultural identity by adapting to outside influences. They created their own chiefly institutions based on the Lunda model. From the Portuguese they adopted new concepts of wealth and

The Chokwe have always drawn on and adapted to outside influences. This Chokwe chief's throne, now in a museum in Luanda, Angola, is based on the shape of early Portuguese chairs. However, the detailed carvings of scenes from Chokwe life transform the chair into a unique Chokwe item. Such Chokwe thrones were symbols of chiefs' power and authority.

political power. As in the case of other African peoples, the Chokwe's success and survival resulted from their cultural flexibility and ability to adapt.

In recent times, however, the Chokwe have had to face many new challenges. Since the early 1970s the Chokwe (and other peoples) have been living amidst civil wars in Angola and Congo. These political conflicts turned the Chokwe territories into battlegrounds. Many displaced Chokwe still live in refugee camps where they wait until they can return safely to their homelands.

Democratic elections in Zambia have brought better living conditions for Chokwe and related peoples living there. The Chokwe in Angola and the neighboring Congo are no longer experiencing civil war, but their countries still face great political problems.

Although Chokwe and related peoples have been greatly affected by modern conflicts, they continue to pursue their own ways. In militarized areas of Angola and Congo, as well as in Zambian refugee camps, they practice initiation, divination, and healing rites. Some Chokwe chiefs have been displaced by war, and their authority has been challenged by modern governments' political goals. Nevertheless, Chokwe chiefs continue to represent traditional and sacred authority.

▼ CHRISTIAN INFLUENCE ▼

The presence of Christian missionaries in Angola since the 1600s has influenced Chokwe culture in different ways. Historically, some missionaries worked with the colonial government to take control over African people and to exploit their labor and natural resources. These resources included precious stones, metals, rubber, and oil.

The missionaries used several different approaches to convert the Chokwe to Christianity. Some forced people to repent and stop their "evil" traditions; others tried to understand Chokwe culture and religious views. Missionaries with the second approach did not impose the Christian faith, but rather offered it to the Chokwe. They found similarities between the Christian and Chokwe religions. For example, both believe in a Supreme Being. Some of the earliest accounts of Chokwe and related peoples come from missionaries.

Today missionaries and Christian churches continue to influence the Chokwe and related peoples. Though many Chokwe have converted to Christianity, most continue their traditional religious practices. Others combine aspects of both Christian and traditional Chokwe religions.

Some churches do not approve of *mukanda* (boys' initiation) camps but allow circumcision in hospitals. These churches accept a period of

Like other people throughout the world, many Chokwe today seek new ways to treasure and support their cultural heritage while taking part in the global community. Seen above is Americo Antonio Kwononoka, the Director of Educational Programs at the Anthropology Museum in Luanda. A historian, he teaches the community about the traditional culture of the Chokwe and other Angolan peoples.

seclusion from the village but forbid traditional ceremonies and masquerades. While most *mikanda* (the plural of *mukanda*) continue to be performed in the traditional way, the Christian version is equally respected in Chokwe villages, and the initiates are allowed to visit the traditional camps.

In the same way, the presence of doctors and modern medicine has challenged the role of diviners and traditional healers. For many Chokwe, though, modern and traditional medicine are not at odds with each other. Most Chokwe will visit both the traditional healer and the hospital if possible. This is because they believe that either a doctor or a healer may diagnose and treat a disease. However, only a diviner can find out the hidden cause of a person's misfortune. Illness may be the result of disharmony with the spiritual world—something that can be revealed only by a diviner.

▼ THE FUTURE ▼

The collective knowledge and experience of the Chokwe, which have been passed down through generations, have helped to create a strong sense of cultural identity. The Chokwe have endured enormous difficulties but their ceremonies continue to celebrate life and renewal. The birth of a child, the full moon, and the changes of the seasons are all viewed by the

Many Chokwe live in modern cities in Angola, Congo, and
Zambia. Seen here is a view of Luanda, the Angolan capital.

Chokwe as signs of a positive future. Most Chokwe continue to overcome problems and to build upon their cultural heritage.

While most Chokwe live in rural areas, many others have moved to the cities. City life is difficult for most Chokwe. They must live in crowded buildings alongside others who have left their lands to escape the horrors of war. Many Chokwe have managed to improve their living conditions, overcoming poverty through education, hard work, and initiative.

As schoolteachers, university students, government officials, and business owners, many Chokwe men and women contribute to the development of the countries in which they live. They maintain their Chokwe cultural identity while contributing to the future of their countries as Angolan, Congolese, and Zambian citizens.▲

Glossary

chimbanda A healer.

chota A shelter where men meet and visitors are received.

divination Process through which the spiritual causes of a problem are revealed.

initiation Process through which people become adults and gain specialized knowledge.

kachipango Shrine for ancestral worship.

Lweji First female Lunda chief.

mahamba Ancestral spirit.

mukanda Male initiation.

mukishi Ancestral spirit in the form of a mask.

tribute A payment by a weak nation to a stronger one for protection.

tupele Symbolic objects tossed in basket during divination sessions.

ukule Female initiation.

uloji A witch or evildoer with supernatural abilities.

For Further Reading

The few sources that exist on the Chokwe are challenging reading.

Bastin, Marie-Louise. *La Sculpture tshokwe.* (English and French). Meudon: Chaffin Editions, 1982.

Jordán, Manuel. "Heavy Stuff and Heavy Staffs from the Chokwe and Related Peoples of Angola, Zaire and Zambia." In *Staffs of Life,* edited by Allen Roberts. Iowa City: University of Iowa Museum of Art, 1994.

Nooter Roberts, Mary. *Secrecy: African Art that Conceals and Reveals.* New York: Museum for African Art, 1993.

Roberts, Allen F. *Animals in African Art: From the Familiar to the Marvelous.* New York: Museum for African Art, 1995.

Roy, Christopher. *Art and Life in Africa: Selections from the Stanley Collection.* Iowa City: University of Iowa Museum of Art, 1992.

Turner, Victor. *The Forest of Symbols.* Ithaca, N.Y.: Cornell University Press, 1982.

Index

ABOUT THE AUTHOR

Manuel Jordán holds a B.A. degree from the University of Puerto Rico in Humanities and both an M.A. and a Ph.D. in Art History from the University of Iowa. He teaches African, Pre-Columbian, and Native American Art at the University of Alabama in Birmingham. He is also the curator of the Arts of Africa and the Americas collection at the Birmingham Museum of Art.

Dr. Jordán has conducted over two years of field research among the Chokwe and related peoples in Zambia and has pursued research at the University of Zambia and the Anthropology Museum in Luanda, Angola. He has published several articles on the Chokwe and related peoples. His latest book, *Maskishi: Masks of the Upper Zambezi River Basin*, will be published in Munich, Germany, in 1998.

PHOTO CREDITS
All photos taken or supplied by the author.

CONSULTING EDITOR AND LAYOUT
Gary N. van Wyk, Ph.D.

SERIES DESIGN
Kim Sonsky